DUNCAN TONATIUH

DANZA!

Amalia Hernández and El Ballet Folklórico de México

ABRAMS BOOKS FOR YOUNG READERS · NEW YORK

Amalia (ah-MAH-lee-ah) Hernández was born in Mexico City in 1917, and everyone assumed she would grow up to be a schoolteacher like her mother and her grandmother. Even Ami (AH-me), as everyone called her, expected that.

But one afternoon while her family was on vacation, Ami saw a pair of dancers in a town square. They stomped and swayed to the live music. The *danzas* that they performed had been danced by people of that area for generations. Ami was hooked. She made a decision: she was going to become a dancer herself.

Ami twirled in the living room and whirled in the kitchen. "Amalia!" scolded her father, a stern military man. But her mother encouraged Ami's interest in the arts, and one day her father gave in. He had a studio built in their home and hired the best dance teachers he could find.

After school, Ami studied ballet with Madame Dambré, who had danced with the Paris Opera, and with Professor Zybin, who had danced with Pavlova's world-renowned Russian ballet.

Ami worked on her technique and made sure she always pointed her feet. She perfected the different structured positions and became an accomplished ballerina.

first

arabesque

fifth

pirouette

grand battement

In 1939, two dancers from the United States visited Mexico City, where Ami lived. They performed a new style of dance called "modern." Amalia was deeply impressed. The movements were expressive, and they could be jarring when compared with the delicate movements of ballet.

Ami met Waldeen, one of the modern dancers, and began to study with her. She also continued practicing ballet. Ami was very talented and disciplined. In time she became a dance teacher and a choreographer herself. A choreographer is a person who creates dance steps and arranges them together to create new dance pieces.

In 1952, after rehearsing for months, Ami and other dancers gave a performance. They presented many different dances, but the one the audience clapped for the most was a piece called *Sones de Michoacán*. Ami was the choreographer, and the dance was similar to the regional *danza* that she had seen in the town square when she was a little girl.

Ami had an idea! She decided that she would create ballets based on the folkloric *danzas* from the different regions of Mexico. She was so excited that she formed her own company with seven other dancers.

Ami began to travel to villages all around the country to learn as much as she could about the area's traditional dances. She read about the history of each place and talked with elders. When possible, she participated in the *danzas* herself. She paid special attention to the steps, the music, and the outfits the people wore.

After returning home, Ami would go to the dance studio. The *danzas y bailes* she saw in the villages were for ceremonial purposes, like celebrating a patron saint or hoping for a good harvest. Other times, the dances happened so people could have fun and meet new friends.

However, the dance pieces Ami was creating were meant to be performances, for audiences to watch in a theater. Ami used her skills as a choreographer and her knowledge of both ballet and modern dance to make the pieces innovative and beautiful. She made sure the dancers wore dazzling costumes, and that there was dramatic lighting and spectacular backdrops.

Audiences loved the folkloric ballets, and Amalia's dance company quickly became very famous. In 1954, they performed on the *Función de Gala* television show. They danced on the show every week for more than sixty weeks! The company grew to include twenty dancers, and then fifty.

The company's repertoire, or stock of dances, included ballets based on *mestizo bailes*, like the *sones jarochos* from Veracruz. Mestizo is the combination of Amerindian, European, and African traditions. In this ballet, musicians dressed in white played the harp and guitars as the dancers stomped on a *tarima*.

15

The company's repertoire also included ballets based on indigenous *danzas*, like *La Danza del Venado* from the Yaqui in the Sonoran Desert . . .

and *Los Quetzales* from the Nahuas and Totonaco people in the Valley of Mexico.

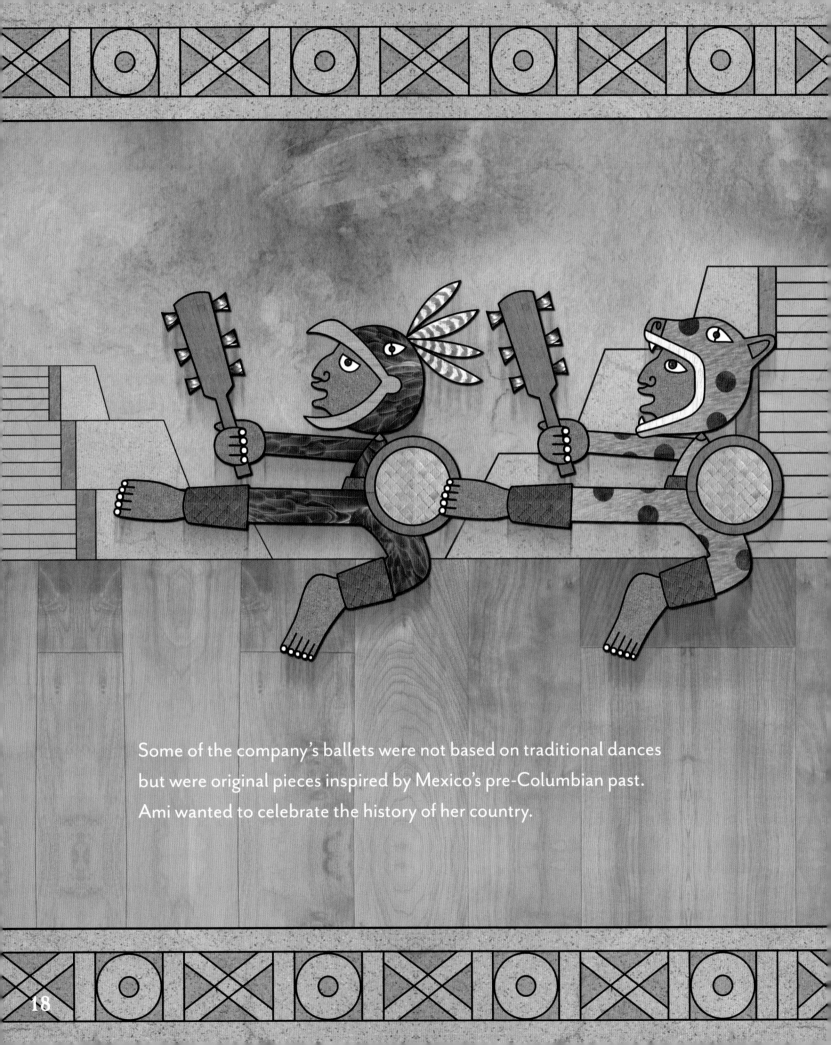

Some of the company's ballets were not based on traditional dances but were original pieces inspired by Mexico's pre-Columbian past. Ami wanted to celebrate the history of her country.

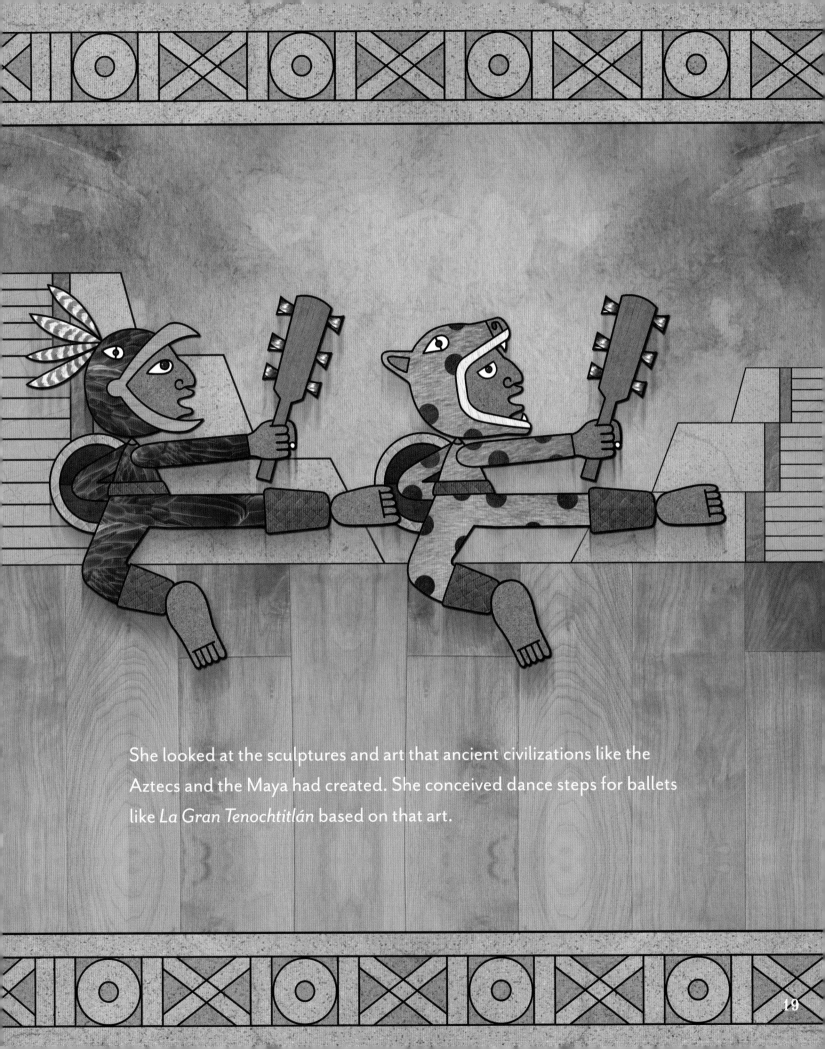

She looked at the sculptures and art that ancient civilizations like the
Aztecs and the Maya had created. She conceived dance steps for ballets
like *La Gran Tenochtitlán* based on that art.

Some ballets were inspired by more recent history and by music like the polka and waltz, which were popular with the wealthy in the nineteenth century.

Or by *corridos*, which were popular with the poor at the beginning of the
twentieth century. Ami would often dance as Juana Gallo, a fierce female

The company became a great success not only in Mexico but abroad, too. In 1959, the Mexican government asked it to represent Mexico in the Pan-American Games. These games are similar to the Olympics, but only athletes from the Americas compete. It was a great honor to be a part of such an important event. That year, Ami decided to call the company *El Ballet Folklórico de México*, Mexico's Folkloric Ballet.

The company became truly international in 1961, when it won the first
prize at the prestigious Festival of Nations in Paris. Famous ballets and
important dance troupes from all over the world competed at the event.
After the Folkloric Ballet won, it was invited to tour in Europe. Later on
it visited Japan and Australia. The dancers even performed next to the
Great Sphinx in Egypt!

To be touring the world was exciting for Ami, but it was not simple to arrange. The company needed transportation for fifty or so dancers, musicians, and sound and lighting technicians . . . and more than three tons of costumes! Ami decided to stop dancing so she could focus on choreographing and directing the company.

She was now like a general, much like her military father, supervising all the different people involved in the Folkloric Ballet and making sure the shows came out perfectly. The company had so many engagements that Ami had to create two groups: one to travel around the world and one to offer performances in Mexico.

In 1968, Ami opened a dance school. Her brother, who was an architect, designed the building, which housed studios and classrooms. At the school, students could learn folkloric dance and also ballet and modern dance. Often the dancers who studied at the school became professionals in Amalia's company.

As the years passed, Ami continued teaching and supervising the Folkloric Ballet's rehearsals. She had become a schoolteacher after all, like her mother and her grandmother.

Amalia Hernández passed away on November 5, 2000, but her legacy lives on. *El Ballet Folklórico de México* performs every Wednesday and Saturday at the *Palacio de Bellas Artes*, the Palace of Fine Arts, in Mexico City. They have been doing so without interruption for more than fifty years! The company also continues to tour internationally.

Today there are thousands of Mexican folkloric dance groups—both professional and amateur—in Mexico and the United States. Perhaps you've seen one perform at your school or in your neighborhood for Cinco de Mayo. Maybe you've even dressed as a *charro* and danced *El Jarabe Tapatío*. I know I have! Ami inspired generations of dancers to perform these *danzas*. She made the folkloric dances of Mexico known around the world, and she encouraged people of Mexican origin to feel pride in their roots and in their traditional dances.

Author's Note

Amalia Hernández's Ballet Folklórico de México is the most famous dance company in Mexico and one of the most famous and successful of its kind in the world. The company has received more than two hundred awards and has performed in more than eighty countries.

Amalia founded her company in 1952. At the time, important Mexican muralists, composers, and writers were finding inspiration for their art in the traditions and history of their country. The Mexican government encouraged this. With the support of President López Mateos and several national institutions, Amalia's Folkloric Ballet quickly became a cultural ambassador for Mexico. When foreign presidents and dignitaries visited the country, the ballet performed for them. On occasion, the ballet also performed abroad for important political figures, as in 1962, when they danced for President John F. Kennedy at the White House. More than sixty years after it was founded, the company continues to champion the folklore and dances of Mexico around the world.

It was not always easy; there were times when Amalia had to put her jewelry and even her father's car up for sale to ensure the financial stability of the company. And at times she was criticized for appropriating and misrepresenting the folkloric dances of Mexico. She was always clear about her intentions, though—namely, to preserve and capture the spirit of traditional dances, which exist for ceremonial or social purposes, and adapt them so they can be enjoyed in a theater. During her life Amalia choreographed more than forty ballets that incorporated local dance traditions from nearly sixty regions.

Folkloric dance is a part of most people's lives in Mexico. Many people partake in local festivities where dance is an integral part of the celebrations. Others, especially children, perform folkloric dances on special occasions. I remember dressing like a *charro* and dancing the *jarabe tapatío* on Mother's Day when I was in elementary school.

In the United States, folkloric dance has a very important role, too. It is a way for people of diverse backgrounds to affirm their heritage. For instance, I cannot imagine a Cinco de Mayo celebration that does not include Mexican American dancers swaying and stomping to the sound of the mariachis. I decided to make this book to learn more about the different folkloric dances of Mexico and to celebrate the person who brought them to the world stage and dedicated her life to them.

Glossary

bailes (BAH-ee-les)—Dances, primarily those done for fun in social gatherings.

ballet—A type of performance dance that originated in Europe in the fifteenth century. Ballet technique is considered the foundation for several other types of dance. The word "ballet" is often used to refer to a dance company, as in the New York City Ballet (company), or to a dance piece, as in "Ami choreographed ballets (dance pieces) inspired in indigenous dances."

charro (CHAH-roh)—A type of horseman, similar to a cowboy.

Cinco de Mayo (SEEN-koh deh MAH-yoh)—May fifth—a celebration that commemorates the unlikely victory of the Mexican army over the powerful invading French army in 1862. The holiday is more popular in the United States than in Mexico; it has become a day in which Mexican American people celebrate their heritage.

corridos (koh-REE-dos)—A type of popular song that tells a story, similar to a ballad.

danza (DAN-zah)—A dance that is performed for an audience or one that has ceremonial purposes.

La Danza del Venado (lah DAN-zah del veh-NAH-doh)—The deer dance, a ceremonial dance from the Yaqui in the Sonoran Desert, in which the main dancer acts like a deer that is being hunted.

folkloric—The traditional beliefs and customs of a community that are passed from generation to generation.

Función de Gala (foon-see-ON deh GAH-lah)—A variety show on television. The name can be translated as *The Gala* or *The Premier Show*.

La Gran Tenochtitlán (teh-noch-tee-TLAN)—The Great Tenochtitlan was the capital city of the Aztec empire, located in what is today Mexico City.

El Jarabe Tapatío (el hah-RAH-beh tah-pah-TEE-oh)—A dance from Jalisco (hah-LEES-koh), a western state in Mexico. It is one of the most famous Mexican dances, both nationally and internationally. Abroad it is often called "The Mexican Hat Dance," because during the dance the male dancer drops his hat on the floor and flirts with the female dancer. At the end of the dance the female picks up the hat signaling that she has accepted the male dancer's advances.

jarochos (hah-ROH-chos)—This term refers to the people of Veracruz. The traditional *jarocho* male outfit is white shirt, white pants, white hat, and a red bandana around the neck.

Juana Gallo (who-AH-nah GAH-yoh)—Juana is a proper name. Gallo can be a last name (it means rooster)—which illustrates how fierce this female soldier was.

Michoacán (me-cho-ah-KHAN)—A state in western Mexico that borders the Pacific Ocean.

Nahuas (NAH-was)—An indigenous group from the Valley of Mexico.

Palacio de Bellas Artes (pah-LAH-cee-oh deh BEH-jas AR-tehs)—The Palace of Fine Arts, a building in downtown Mexico City, completed in 1934. El Ballet Folklórico de México has been performing there for more than fifty years. The palace houses several famous murals and hosts acclaimed operas, orchestras, and exhibits on a regular basis.

polka—A category of music and a type of dance that originated in central Europe in the middle of the nineteenth century.

quetzales (ket-ZAH-les)—Birds with bright green feathers that can be found in areas of Mexico and in Central America.

son / sones (sohn / SOH-nes)—*Son* is a type of Latin American music. Mexican *son* is usually played with guitars and other string instruments. Dancers of Mexican *son* often stomp on the floor or on a wood platform to give the music percussion and rhythm.

Sonoran Desert a desert that covers large parts of Arizona and California in the United States, and large parts of the states of Sonora and Baja California Norte and Sur in Mexico.

tarima (tah-REE-mah)—A wood platform on which dancers stomp.

Totonaco (toh-TOH-nah-coh)—An indigenous group from the eastern coastal and mountainous region of Mexico.

Veracruz (veh-rah-CRUISE)—A state in eastern Mexico that borders the Gulf of Mexico.

waltz—A slow, elegant dance that became popular with the European upper class in the eighteenth century and later with the upper class in other parts of the world.

Yaqui (JAH-key)—An indigenous group from the Sonoran Desert.

Bibliography

BOOKS

Aguirre Cristiani, Gabriela, and Felipe Segura Escalona. *El Ballet Folklórico de México de Amalia Hernández*. Mexico City: Fomento Cultural Banamex, 1994.

Shay, Anthony. *Choreographing Politics: State Folk Dance Companies, Representation and Power*. Middletown, Conn.: Wesleyan University Press, 2002.

DOCUMENTARIES

Krauze, Enrique. *Amalia Hernández, El espectáculo de la danza*. Mexico City: Clío TV, 2000

Urias, Patricia. *Retrato Intimo, Amalia Hernández*. Mexico City: XEIPN Canal Once, 2002

WEBSITES AND ARTICLES

www.balletfolkloricodemexico.com.mx
www.uam.mx/difusion/revista/feb2002/tortajada.html
articles.latimes.com/2000/nov/05/local/me-47382

INTERVIEWS

Informal interviews in 2016 with Marylin Arrieta, who danced with the Folkloric Ballet in the early 1960s under the stage name Xóchitl Maguey.

Index

Note: Page numbers in *italics* refer to illustrations.

To Mary, Marylin, Patty, Vida and to all my dancers! Work!

The art in this book was hand-drawn, then collaged digitally.

Cataloging-in-Publication Data has been applied for and may be obtained from the Library of Congress.
ISBN: 978-1-4197-2532-6

Text and illustrations copyright © 2017 Duncan Tonatiuh
Book design by Julia Marvel

Printed and bound in China
10 9 8 7 6 5 4 3 2

Abrams Books for Young Readers are available at special discounts when purchased in quantity for premiums and promotions as well as fundraising or educational use. Special editions can also be created to specification. For details, contact specialsales@abramsbooks.com or the address below.

ABRAMS The Art of Books
195 Broadway, New York, NY 10007
abramsbooks.com